A Sexagenarian From Smithy Fen,
and Other Limericks

Valerie Fish

Copyright © 2021 Valerie Fish
All rights reserved.
ISBN: 978-1-9168926-0-6

A Sexagenarian From Smithy Fen

A Sexagenarian From Smithy Fen,
and Other Limericks

CONTENTS

Acknowledgments i

A Sexagenarian from Smithy Fen... 1

Where Am I? 2

Parlez vous Français? 4

News Headlines 6

Famous Faces..11

Giving In, Giving Up 16

Don't Panic! 17

A Trio of Naughty Clergymen 19

Ooh Matron! 20

Playing Away... 25

Right Royal Tales... 26

Tales of the Unexpected	28
Tits and Bits!	29
Wedding Bells	37
Poor Hubby	39
Merry Christmas…	41
… and a Happy New Year	42
This Is Me…	43
About the Author	45
More Writing from Valerie	46

Acknowledgments

This collection of my limericks would not have been possible without the encouragement and support of my fellow Whittlesey Wordsmiths. Particular thanks go to Phil, for his confidence in me, and persuading me to take the plunge, Cathy for her editing and formatting, Jane for her brilliant illustrations, and Val C for her kind words.

A Sexagenarian from Smithy Fen...

A sexagenarian from Smithy Fen
Was dallying with three different men.
After every date
Performance she'd rate
Awarding them marks out of ten.

I don't normally start my limericks in the conventional way, but now that I have your attention….

Well, I am a sexagenarian who lives in the Fens, but romance-wise, there is only one man in my life (thankfully!) my dear hubby of forty-five years.

I have been writing limericks for as long as I can remember; many of my efforts have been published In the Daily Mail. My ideas often come from something in the news, or I will take up a prompt or first line given in an online challenge. Sometimes they are simply a reflection of me.

So, welcome to my world of limericks, and I hope they can raise a smile or two.

Valerie

Where Am I?

    A young fellow from Market Deeping
    Had a nasty habit while sleeping.
    His somnambulation
    Caused great consternation;
    Through women's windows he was peeping!

A friend of mine from Cornwall, a local councillor, remarked 'You should try Mevagissey.'
Always up for a challenge, I came up with…

    A budding politician from Meva
    Cried, 'Me, write a limerick? Never!
    I haven't the time
    To think of a rhyme.
    Or maybe I'm just not that clever.'

Before you accuse me of cheating, 'Meva' is what it's known as by the locals.
Just a few miles away lies the village of Trewhiddle, but I just couldn't seem to come up with a rhyme!

And a trio of Radio Cambridgeshire entries, with a local town and village as the prompt…

    At a fancy dress do down in Bury,
    Maid Marian had a drop too much sherry.
    It wasn't young Robin
    Who had her heart throbbin';
    'Twas Little John who made Marian merry!

A Radio Cambridgeshire listener from Oldhurst
Each week would try penning a verse,
But time after time
They'd neither scan nor rhyme;
They just went from bad to worse.
                (How not to write a limerick).

A courting young couple from Coates
Loved messing about in boats.
As they sailed on the Cam
They couldn't give a damn
As long as they got their oats!

Parlez vous Français?

French and English were the only subjects I was any good at in my schooldays, and I like to throw in the odd French word or expression…

Late for school, couldn't get out of bed.
I've been summoned to see the head.
In a *fait accompli*
No detention for me.
Sir's been given the sack instead.

He loved to play the connoisseur
Of fine food; a right *bon viveur*.
Though he'd never confess,
When no-one to impress
It's a Maccy D he would prefer.

On a glass-bottomed boat on the Seine
Sharing a bottle of Brut (champagne),
'Eiffel' overboard
For handsome Jean-Claude.
We're honeymooning in sunny Spain!

All it takes is a whiff of 'J'Adore'
To whisk me back to May Seventy-Four.
At the altar, a bride,
And stood by my side,
My wonderful *Cheri Amour*.

He showered her with goodies galore
Posh perfume, jewellery and more.
But she longed for the day
When he'd turn round and say
Those three little words, '*Je t'adore.*'

After Phil's Christmas cracker with Mel,
She decided to kiss and tell
To her best mate Lisa,
Who gunned down the geezer
In a classic *crime passionel.*
                 (EastEnders, Christmas 2000).

Last night we tried *nouvelle cuisine*,
But the portions… boy were they mean.
Forked out loads of dosh
For pretentious nosh.
Tomorrow it's the staff canteen!

News Headlines

Hungry for profit, he's at it again.
O'Leary's idea is simply insane.
In an emergency
Forget duty free;
Your stewardess is flying the plane!

Unbelievable but true...
'Eliminating the co-pilot
'For the executive of an airline, O'Leary doesn't seem too concerned about air safety, suggesting that the standard allotment of two pilots per plane is one too many. "Let's take out the second pilot. Let the bloody computer fly it," he's said.
'Alternatively, he suggested that the flight attendants be trained to fly, so that they could step up to the plate in cases of emergency.'

The Week online, 8 Jan 2105

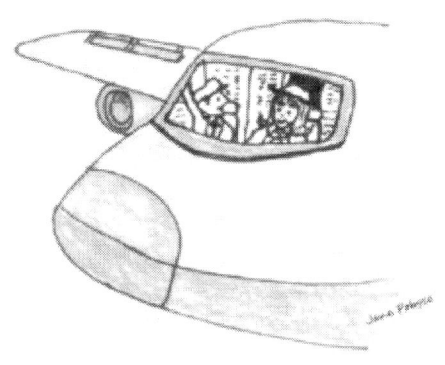

Is it a bird, is it a plane?
Oh no, it's happening again;
Another damn drone
In a no-fly zone.
Disruption all round; what a pain.

'A drone flying close to Gatwick Airport led to the closure of the runway and forced five flights to be diverted.
'An airport spokesman said the runway had been closed for two periods on Sunday - of nine and five minutes - after the drone was sighted.
'Easyjet said four of its flights were diverted, while British Airways said one aircraft was diverted to Bournemouth.
'Other flights were put into holding patterns as a precaution.'
BBC News, 3rd July 2017

A satellite the size of a bus
Is, alarmingly, heading for us.
It will probably
Safely land in the sea.
But should we check with Nostradamus?

'A twenty-year-old satellite the size of a bus has fallen out of orbit and is expected to crash somewhere on Earth next week.
'Scientists have identified twenty-six separate pieces that could survive the fall through the Earth's atmosphere and debris could rain across an area 400 to 500 kilometres wide.'
ABC News, 16th Sep 2011

Can you believe the latest craze
For mums on the school run these days?
Forget, 'dress to impress',
Rather, 'Oh what a mess',
Still wearing slippers and PJ's.

'A headteacher has written to parents to request that they do not wear pyjamas and slippers to take children to and from school.
'The teacher requests that parents take the time to dress appropriately in day wear which is suitable for the weather conditions.'

Teesside Gazette, 26 Jan 2016

The PM has pledged there will be
For over 40's, a health MOT.
But I've parts need replacing;
Engine failure I'm facing.
I fear it's the scrap heap for me.

'New health checks for the over-40s, which the government claims could save 650 lives a year, are being introduced by the NHS in England today.
'The "health MOTs" are part of a range of new measures that include MRSA screening in hospitals and free prescriptions for cancer patients.'

The Guardian, 1st Apr 2009
(...and no, this wasn't an April Fool!)

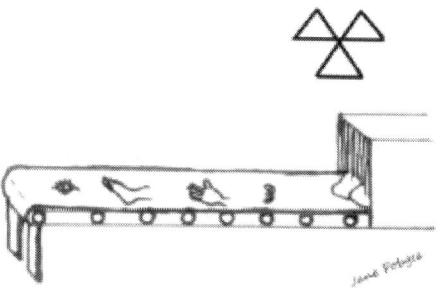

The production turned out such a scream,
With global scenes of violence extreme.
Titus Andronicus
Scared the hell out of us.
Wasn't quite A Midsummer Night's Dream.

'Scenes of rape, mutilation and murder have earned it a reputation as the Bard's bloodiest play. And at Tuesday night's performance of Titus Andronicus, one gruesome moment brought audience members to their knees.
'As Lavinia, whose tongue and hands are cut off after she is raped, appeared on stage at Shakespeare's Globe, five people fainted. Others complained of feeling sick and fearing sleepless nights.'
Daily Mail, 1 May 2014

Back when flower power was at its height,
Nineteen sixty-eight, Isle of Wight,
'Make love not war,' I declared
With everything bared.
Just turned fifty, the fruits of that night!

'Often regarded as the UK's equivalent to Woodstock, the Isle of Wight Festival embodied the spirit of the flower power generation when it launched in 1968. No one could have ever imagined rock greats such as Jimi Hendrix and Jefferson Airplane would perform on a tiny island popular with retirees. But every summer, for three consecutive years, the Solent's holiday idyll was swept up in a whirlwind of rock 'n' roll hedonism.'
Belfast Telegraph, 8th Jun 2018
Tickets were then twenty-five shillings (the equivalent of £1.25 today).

Have you ever heard such a fuss?
Poor Granny got kicked off the bus.
What caused her expulsion?
A tin of emulsion.
Should the shade have been strawberry blush?

'A grandmother travelling on a bus with her four-year-old granddaughter has hit out after being kicked off for carrying a pot of paint. They say the driver started shouting that he was not insured to carry paint and even threatened calling police.'

Daily Express, Apr 21st, 2017

Jane Pobgee

Famous Faces

Mesmerised and unable to speak,
I'm feeling decidedly weak.
Glued to the telly,
My legs turned to jelly
At the sight of Poldark's physique.

Jade found her fame on Big Brother:
A reality star like no other.
A life cut short;
A brave battle fought
By, at heart, loving wife and mother.

On the Spice Girls' first night back on tour
The sound system was causing a stir.
But some people might say,
At the end of the day
Their sound wasn't that great before.

(With apologies to Neil)
'The Spice Girls reunion tour has been hit with complaints and demands for refunds.'

The Independent 28 May 2019

And now for today's weather forecast….

> Michael Fish was too quick to allay
> Fears of a hurricane on its way.
> Untold damage was done
> (Sevenoaks became one)
> When the great storm hit later that day.

Being married to a Michael Fish, we've had our fair share of witty remarks over the years. 'Michael Fish?' They grin, and more often or not the word 'hurricane' will be mentioned.
But what they don't know is, my father was in the Met Office, and knew *that* Michael Fish personally. Dad could have been a forecaster for the BBC himself but didn't fancy the fame.
Nowadays the forecasts are presented by any old body…

> I have to confess that I'm smitten
> With Piers on *Good Morning Britain*.
> As brash as he seems,
> I bet the man of my dreams
> Underneath is as soft as a kitten.

> Her candle burned out long ago,
> The beautiful Marilyn Monroe.
> I'd sit glued to the screen,
> Bewitched by Norma Jean
> And wishing I was Joe DiMaggio.

He craftily wore a disguise;
He'd not see his kids otherwise.
Donning female attire,
Darling Mrs Doubtfire
Made us laugh and brought tears to our eyes.

Poor Bean, how he felt such a fool
When losing his trunks in the pool.
With nowhere to hide
He swallowed his pride,
Emerged clutching his tiny tool.

On our TV screens he soon became
A hugely admired household name.
He's with us no more,
But up there I'm sure
Brucie's still crying, 'Good game, good game!'

First encountered at Paddington station
And oft a cause of consternation,
For five decades
His escapades
Have charmed and captivated the nation.

While on my mobile phone,
A voice from the unknown
Cried out, 'I'm lost.
My wires are crossed.'
It was ET, phoning home!

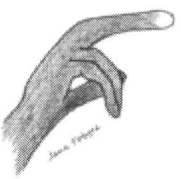

For any *Friends* fans, from someone who knows practically every line from the complete series...

The truth was just too hard to take
He couldn't admit his mistake.
Ross just kept repeating
'It's not really cheating,'
To Rachel. 'We were on a break!'

'Sexual relations did not take place!'
Said Bill Clinton, pleading his case.
But his DNA
Gave him away
As plain as the nose on his face.

As the apple fell from the tree,
Newton cried out excitedly,
'If my theory's right,
I think I just might
Have discovered gravity.'

'Twas the ladies' night out in Rhyl
With everyone dressed to kill.
Seats in the front row,
Spare knickers in tow.
Tom Jones was topping the bill!

Giving In, Giving Up

I'm forever trying to diet
But frequently, 'dying to try it'.
When a cream cake cries, 'Eat me!'
Temptation defeats me.
I just go right ahead and buy it.

I've tried and I've failed every year,
But this time I will persevere.
January will be
A dry one for me.
First of Feb, I'll be back on the beer.

For Lent, I have given up booze,
But I've got a bad case of the blues.
A large G and T
Cries out, 'Drink me, drink me!'
It's an offer I cannot refuse.

Don't Panic!

My phobia has plagued me for years.
They say you must confront your fears
But, try as I might,
I have to take flight
Each time Incy Wincy appears.

This phobia's becoming a pain
The minute I set foot on a plane
I scream and I shout,
'Let me out, let me out!'
As aerophobia strikes again.

Which leads to...

We should be sunning ourselves in Spain,
But I let everyone down yet again.
I must persevere
And conquer my fear;
One day I will get on that plane.

And it's not just us humans that suffer…
For Nicky, Eli, and Peppa.

Lay quivering in his bed
Blanket pulled over his head.
'Whizz bang and pop,
'Please make them stop.
I'm waiting for walkies,' he said.

A Trio of Naughty Clergymen

With his sermon about to begin
The priest had to suppress a huge grin,
'Cos just minutes ago,
Out the back with a pro,
He'd committed a cardinal sin.

Forgive me father, I concede
I have sinned in thought word and deed
With Sister Theresa.
She begged me to please 'er.
The poor girl was in desperate need.

Tired of living a life of vice
She went to her priest for advice.
'You must renounce your sin
But before you begin,
One last performance would be nice.'

Ooh Matron!

And carrying on in that vein, a bunch of my bawdier efforts to tickle your fancy...

To the missus I tried to suggest,
'A change is as good as a rest.
A threesome would be
A nice novelty.'
Such a shame that she wasn't impressed.

The shame she would never forget;
She'd done something rash for a bet.
Her spectacular boob
Was now out on You Tube
With ten thousand hits as of yet.

Temptation's a terrible sin.
I can't let that old devil win.
I must try harder
To curb my ardour,
The trouble I've got myself in!

We used to do it three times a week
But now our sex life's passed its peak.
She's lost her ardour;
It's time to try harder
And impress with a new technique.

We'd never had such a huge fight;
We were at it well into the night.
Boy, was making up fun.
A new life begun,
Nine months later, our little mite.

Under the boardwalk of Brighton pier
A drunken encounter cost me dear.
I gave him my all
Up against the wall.
The little 'un's due early next year.

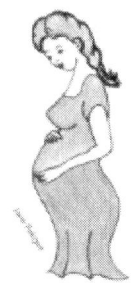

I just couldn't believe my eyes;
I have never seen such a size.
There was no topping
Her melons so whopping.
She waltzed off with 'Best in Class' prize.

Whilst reading *Fifty Shades of Grey*
On your morning commute, you may
Turn fifty shades of red
At their antics in bed.
It was never like that in my day!

She'd a brain the size of a pea,
Her cup size, a huge double-D.
She wasn't so dumb.
Success was to come
Flaunting her assets on Page Three.

A woman was dating three guys,
Measuring each one up for size.
It wasn't the longest
Who finished the strongest.
Little Rod romped home with first prize.

I fancy a nice bit of tart,
But I should really think of my heart.
The excitement could see
An early exit for me…
But what a great way to depart.

I wasn't convinced she was 'game',
But I made my pass just the same.
She soon cried 'foul'
And began to howl.
I had only myself to blame.

In the mile high club, she often flew,
All business conducted in the loo,
Emerging quite flushed
To looks of disgust
From desperate folk waiting in the queue.

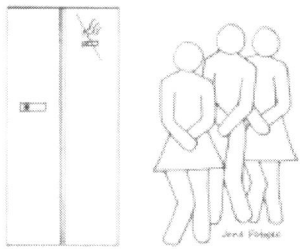

In their open top automobile
A couple could hardly conceal
Their state of undress,
But couldn't care less
Caught in flagrante behind the wheel.

I have never felt so betrayed.
Just found out my boyfriend has laid
My identical twin.
His defence, (somewhat thin)
'It's a mix-up easily made.'

I once went on a date with a cop
Who'd a penchant for women on top.
But when his truncheon
Failed to function,
You could say the whole thing was a flop.

Said the dentist, clutching his drill,
'Now just open wide and sit still.
First a tiny prick
That should do the trick.
You won't feel a thing – but I will!'

Playing Away

The old witch was out like a light.
My chance to escape for the night
For stolen kisses
With my mate's missus
And back home in bed before light.

I found proof of my fella's affair:
A black peephole brassiere
And Brazilian thong
Where they didn't belong,
And a tell-tale strand of a stranger's hair.

Honeymoon suite all booked at The Grand,
Every detail meticulously planned.
I'd not bargained for
A knock at the door:
The missus, divorce papers in hand.

An affair may seem like a thrill.
Trust me, it's a given, you will
Rue the day
You played away
When handed a huge divorce bill.

Right Royal Tales

When Henry and Anne of Cleves wed
Things fell short in the marital bed.
A sorry affair
For the Flanders Mare
But at least she got to keep her head!

Their affair was the talk of the town,
But when the king gave up his crown
For a yank twice divorced
And who looked like a horse,
Edward let the whole nation down.

The duchess had herself a new beau
Who delighted in sucking her toe.
Ensuing pics X-rated
Left her humiliated,
And the queen crying, 'She's got to go!'

It was the event of the year.
Will and Kate's wedding brought good cheer.
But I'm tired of hearing
(And my fella's leering)
Of Pippa Middleton's rear.

A two-bit actress sought a prince to marry;
Set her sights on our darling Harry.
She whisked him away
From KP to LA,
And now she's as happy as Larry.

Tales of the Unexpected

Little Bo Beep has lost her flock;
They've escaped and run amok.
Now she has to wait
By the wooden gate
That she'd forgotten to lock.

Hare to tortoise, 'Let's cut to the chase,
You've no hope of winning this race.'
But was fated to lose
When he stopped for a snooze
And finished with egg on his face.

Whilst waltzing at a very posh do,
The clock started to strike. Off she flew.
But Cinderella
Landed her fella
When he came calling with matching shoe.

The parade was a grand affair.
The throng couldn't help but just stare.
A boy in the crowd
Had cried out loud,
'The emperor's completely bare!'

Tits and Bits!

...or anything else that doesn't belong anywhere else.

Apologies for the title; this was the name of a shop in Majorca, not selling adult goods, as you might expect, but cheap and tacky tourist souvenirs. We've stayed at the same resort a few times, with fond memories, and for some infantile reason, this always made us smile.

If I win the lottery, for sure
I'd like to donate to the poor.
Kith and kin, though not needy
(but just downright greedy)
Will be queuing up at my door.

We were at the Hollywood Bowl.
I was fit and ready to roll
Till, screaming in pain,
I sailed down the lane
With one finger stuck in a hole.

I've always been useless at sport;
I'm just not the athletic sort.
I'd come last every race,
I couldn't keep pace,
And at long jump, I always fell short.

In a relationship, there must
Be honesty, respect and trust.
His cheating heart
Drove us apart.
Now all my dreams have turned to dust.

In my heart I've a terrible pain.
When can I hug my grandson again?
We're over the peak,
So why not next week?
Before I go completely insane!

He'd never had such a fright,
Turning a deadly shade of white
When mother-in-law,
Who's with us no more,
Came calling that dark stormy night.

Copped a fine, whilst drunk on the train
I pulled the emergency chain.
There's no excuse
For improper use.
Note to self: next time engage brain!

While they were picnicking on the beach,
Mum suddenly let out a huge screech.
From right out of the sky
A greedy gull swung by
And swiftly swooped off with her peach.

I could have said I was confused,
Or a better word could be used,
But I calculated
Discombobulated
Would just leave everybody bemused.

Six feet under, I heard the death knell.
Oh, Dear God, I'd been sentenced to hell.
Thank the Lord I survived
Being buried alive,
'Cos I truly was saved by the bell.

Tomorrow, today's headline, it's said,
Is yesterday's news, and instead
A new juicy story
Grabs front page glory.
Just don't always believe what you've read.

The spellchecker on my PC
Is like a best mate too me.
It's got watt it takes
Two put write my mistakes.
Without it wear wood eye bee?

The email arrived yesterday.
Fantastic news, I've won £10K.
'Just follow this link…'
Do they really think
I'm that stupid? No way José.

My wife's disappeared – don't know where.
I'm in a state of deep despair.
She's left me high and dry
With the washing piled high
And the cupboard's completely bare.

Some people will say that I'm 'sad'.
Winter blues I get really bad.
Birds get to migrate;
I just hibernate,
Cocooned in my warm cosy pad.

I was sick of his constant lies,
All ready to say my goodbyes.
But he turned on the charm;
I was back in his arms,
Seduced by those come-to-bed eyes.

It's been raining all afternoon.
We're needing some sunshine, and soon.
Only one more day
Of a cold wet May.
Let us pray for a flaming June.

30 May 2021

Due to circumstances unforeseen
Val had an abundance of greens.
Her brussels gone rotten,
Parsnips long forgotten,
And as limp as you've ever seen.
(Christmas 2020 for a fellow Whittlesey Wordsmith member).

Tomorrow's the Spring Equinox.
We'll soon see the changing of clocks.
This cold little bunny
Fails to find it funny,
Still clad in thermals and woolly socks.

(Written after a harsh winter that seemed to go on and on forever.)

He'd gone all out to set the right mood:
Soft music and the lighting subdued.
But it all went to pot,
The chilli far too hot.
Several trips to the toilet ensued.

I've just won the lottery: 10K.
I'm planning my dream holiday,
Where it's clear blue seas
And ninety degrees…
Oh no! I've thrown my ticket away.

On the seven-thirty to Crewe,
A commuter was on the loo
When a technical hitch
With the sliding door hitch
Left his business for all to view.

The body lay dead on the floor.
'Twas a horrific sight, for sure.
Hysterical wife
Finds husband with knife.
He'd murdered his mother-in-law.

Our long-awaited cruise on the Seine
Was spoilt by the never-ending rain.
So we all slowly mastered
The art of getting plastered
In Paris again and again.

I've got myself in a right stew.
I'm nauseous and overdue.
I've just peed on a stick;
I'm going to be sick!
Please someone, tell me it's not true...

After eighty-seven years of tradition,
Centre Court's sporting a new addition:
A retractable roof
Making play weatherproof.
All we need now's a win for Great Britain!

17th May 2009

My husband and I were privileged to be in the Centre Court crowd at the unveiling of the new roof, and watch two of my tennis idols, Andre Agassi and Steffi Graff, among others, play some entertaining exhibition matches.
As the roof began to close, Katherine Jenkins and Faryl Smith gave a beautiful rendition of 'Amazing Grace': an experience I'll always treasure.

Andy Murray gave us that long-awaited win four years later in 2013.

Wedding Bells

It was love at first sight for us two.
All it took was one look and we knew.
I met my Mr Right
That memorable night,
And tomorrow we're saying, 'I Do'.

As the best man was toasting the bride
A drunken guest stood up and cried,
'That sweet lass you've wed
Has not just been in my bed
But half the men present, besides.'

The best man was proposing a toast
He just couldn't help but boast.
'Today's stunning bride,'
He drunkenly cried,
'Was yesterday's notch on my bedpost!'

The stag night was simply a hoot.
The groom-to-be, pissed as a newt,
Was found at daybreak,
Tied to a stake,
Wearing nowt but his birthday suit.

Poor Hubby

My poor hubby doesn't often fare well in my limericks, I try to tell him it's called 'poetic licence' but I'm not sure he's convinced.
I do love him really...

'Twas a nightmare, a terrible fright:
Count Dracula was taking a bite.
But then I awoke;
It was hubby's sick joke.
He slept downstairs the rest of the night.

Last night I dreamt of the Azores:
Palm trees, clear blue seas, sun-kissed shores.
Sadly paradise
Was lost in a trice,
Dreams shattered by dear hubby's snores.

It was all planned: a cruise round the Med.
Now, thanks to Covid 19, instead
I'm stuck home on my tod
Whist hubby, the daft sod
Is self-isolating in the shed.

Covid19 and lockdown have meant couples spending more time together and being stuck indoors has caused friction for many. The ladies in my writing group were discussing ways of committing mariticide; one member (who shall remain nameless to spare her blushes) had penned a story with an original choice of a menorah as the murder weapon.

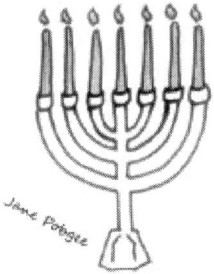

Not to be outdone, I came up with this...

> The new patio's just been laid.
> A heavy price hubby has paid.
> I'm done with his lying;
> There'll be no more crying.
> Oh shit, I've got blood on the spade.

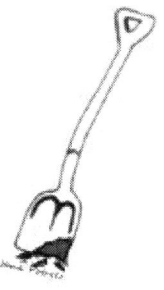

And this is hubby getting his own back...

> The wife's nagging's driving me insane.
> Yesterday she was at it again.
> But there's one thing for sure,
> Now she's dead on the floor,
> That's the last time she'll ever complain.

Merry Christmas...

When it comes to Christmas, I tend
To go crazy and overspend.
But it costs me dear,
'Cos all the next year,
I'm paying back my flexible friend.

(Only those of a certain age will know who I'm talking about.)

Though not always proud of his frame,
His portliness brought him great fame.
His role in Aladdin
Had no need of padding
As the perfect pantomime dame.

The one person I used to revere,
My dear father, is no longer here.
At my window today,
A robin popped by to say,
'Merry Christmas; your loved ones are near.'

... and a Happy New Year

As twenty-twenty draws to a close
What does the future hold? Who knows?
We must all hope and pray
That soon will be the day
This evil Covid gets up and goes.

31 Dec 2020

This Is Me...

I've a brain the size of a pea;
Learning never came easy for me.
But I've a heart of gold
Which is worth, so I'm told,
Far more than some fancy degree.

As previously mentioned, I was never particularly academic. Luckily, I had no lofty ambitions to be a rocket scientist, but the one subject I did love was English Language.

To be publishing a book at my stage of life means such a lot to me, and if you've managed to get this far, I hope it has brought you some pleasure.

Thank you for taking a peek into my world of limericks.

Valerie

If you enjoyed this book, please leave a review online

About the Author

Born and bred in London, Valerie now lives in the Fens with her husband of 45 years.

She has been writing on and off for most of her adult life. Now retired, she has more time to devote to her passion, with renewed enthusiasm since joining her local u3a Creative Writing Group.

She calls herself a 'three in the morning writer', as it's often when tossing and turning in the early hours that inspiration comes, and stories develop.

As well as limericks, she enjoys writing Flash Fiction, particularly 50- or 100-worders, regularly contributing to online challenges and having snippets published in the *Daily Mail*.

Find Valerie online at https://sexegenarianscribbler.wordpress.com/

More Writing from Valerie

Find more limericks, flash fiction and short stories from Valerie in anthologies from the Whittlesey Wordsmiths.

Available from Amazon

A second collection from our writing group

Available from Amazon

Printed in Great Britain
by Amazon